Sportoons

**Gags & Cartoons
by
Larry Lambert & David Carpenter**

**Edited
by
Stan Silliman
Comedy Empire Press**

Comedy Empire Press
3334 W. Main, Suite 126
Norman, OK 73072

ISBN Number: 1-886682-03-8

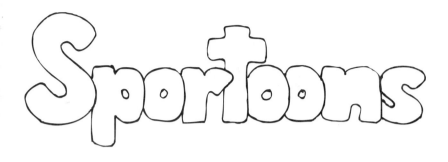

DAVE CARPENTER and LARRY LAMBERT are a true pair of sports nuts. When not cartooning or selling gags, either of this pair can be found on the links, on the courts, on the lanes, or umping or coaching little league. Lambert may be the only umpire to carry a notepad in his back pocket and to sometimes be heard yelling "What did you call me? Really? Could you spell that, please?"

Stan Silliman,
Editor

LARRY LAMBERT's gags have appeared in a number of national publications, including *The Wall Street Journal, Better Homes & Gardens* and *National Review.*

He has also sold to TV stand-ups, including Jay Leno for the *Tonight Show.* For years, he provided a weekly comedy service for radio stations throughout the Southwest. He currently supplies some of the gags for the comic strip *Mother Goose and Grim*, which appears in over 1,000 newspapers nationwide.

As a long-time sports fan, Larry feels humor in sports isn't hard to find; it's just a matter of being objective. Of course an objective sports fan is an oxymoron, as any non sports fan will tell you. So whether you're a sports fan or not, you can enjoy *SPORTOONS*.

Larry lives in Tecumseh, Oklahoma with his wife Nona and sons Quinton and Barak.

DAVE CARPENTER's
cartoons have appeared
in the nation's most
popular and well known
magazines, from *The Wall
Street Journal* to the
Saturday Evening Post.
Readers have seen the
artistry of his wit in *Barron's,
Forbes, National Review, Good
Housekeeping, Better Homes & Gardens, Woman's World*, as
well as in *First, McCalls, Woman's Own, New Woman, Omni,
King Features, National Enquirer, National Business
Employment Weekly, American Management Association,
Rotarian, American Legion, VFW, Kiwanis, Lion* publications.

He began his professional cartoonist career in 1981.

5

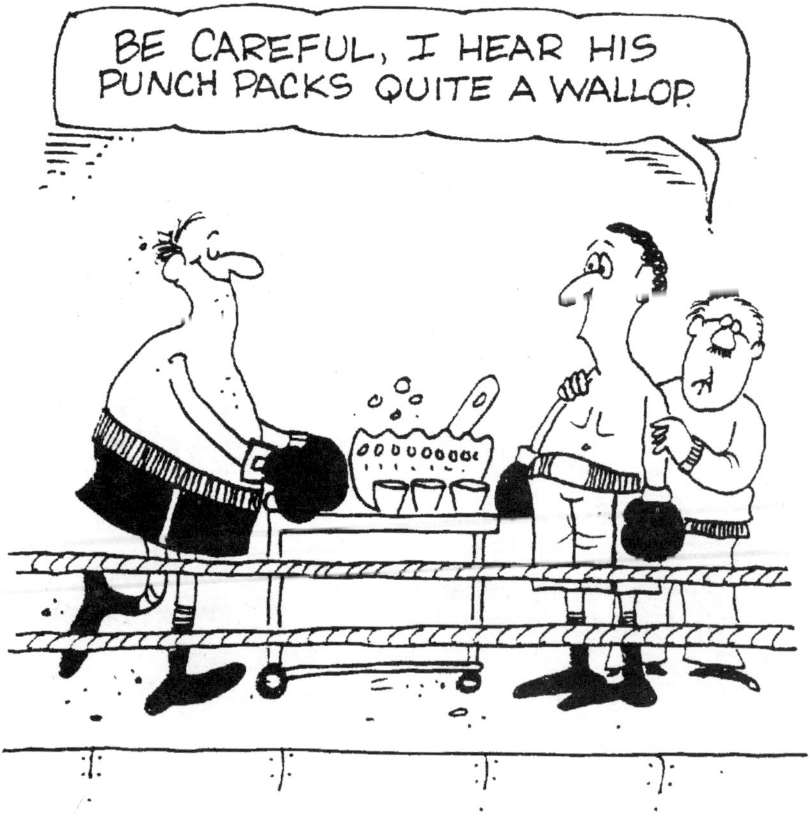
BE CAREFUL, I HEAR HIS PUNCH PACKS QUITE A WALLOP

UNDER RIGHT CONDITIONS —
WHITE MEN CAN JUMP.

"I HATE THE DAY AFTER THE SUPER BOWL."

WHY BASEBALL PLAYERS HATE TO PLAY ON ASTRO TURF DURING HOT WEATHER.

PUTTING ON GAME FACES FOR
MONDAY NIGHT FOOTBALL.

IT'S A LETTER FROM ONE OF OUR ALUMNI. HE SAYS
THERE'S THIS KID NAMED GULLIVER WE SHOULD TAKE
A LOOK AT."

CLAYBOURNE HAD HEARD THAT THE BASEBALLS WERE REALLY JUICED UP THIS SEASON.

15

YOU'D HAVE TO GO PRETTY FAR TO FIND A CADDY AS COMMITTED AS DUANE.

CLAYTON REALIZES THAT HIS CAREER MAY BE ON THE
DOWNSLIDE WHEN HE LEARNS THAT HE'S BEEN TRADED
TO PITTSBURGH———— FOR A CATCHER'S MITT.

CARL BAINLEY, SET A CHANNEL CROSSING RECORD THAT WILL PROBABLY NEVER BE ACHIEVED AGAIN.

'OUR 'NICKEL DEFENSE' ISN'T WORTH TWO CENTS...

21

"NO, NO, DON'T PUT IT DOWN YET..."

23

WHY ROOKIE LEAGUE BASEBALL TRIPS
ARE SUCH A PAIN.

ASSISTANT TRACK COACH ERNIE GATES PREPARES TO WARM-UP THE JAVELIN THROWERS.

FRED MISUNDERSTANDS THE CONCEPT OF
FLY FISHING

"OH, ALRIGHT, YOU CRYBABIES, I'LL CALL THE GAME."

LARRY WAS SO FOCUSED ON CORRELATING THE DISTANCE TO THE PIN, THAT HE DID NOT PAY ATTENTION TO THE SPECIFICS OF THE SAND TRAP.

31

A VIEW FROM INSIDE THE GOLF HOLE

RAPID EXPANSION CAUSED A DILUTION IN THE
SUMO WRESTLING TALENT POOL.

SWANSON FAILS TO FACE REALITY.

"COME ON NOW, CLARK, EVERYONE PLAYS
WITH A LITTLE PAIN."

"CRENSHAW, YOU'RE GONNA BE BLOCKING # 71 ..."

UNION LEADER, BOB WILLIAMS, DISPLAYS GOOD COMMAND OF THE STRIKE ZONE.

"WOW! QUITE A CAMOUFLAGE OUTFIT, ED."

WES JOHNSON IS A **POINT** GUARD IN MORE WAYS THAN ONE.

42

"ED STRAINED AN EYEBALL WHILE USING THAT NEW, SUPER MODELS WORKOUT TAPE."

"...AND HE HAS A LIFETIME RECORD
OF 3-2, IN SALARY ARBITRATION..."

YEARS OF HEADERS HAD TAKEN THEIR TOLL ON SOCCER GREAT, PABLO PEREZ.

47

"YES, THIS IS WHERE THE MARATHON FINISHED,
BUT THAT WAS THREE DAYS AGO."

LONG TIME SUBSTITUTE, WENDELL REARDON, FINALLY GETS CALLED INTO A GAME.

"FOR THOSE OF YOU WHO MISSED THE T.V. BLOOPERS
SHOW LAST NIGHT, HERE'S THE FILM FROM OUR LAST
GAME."

WHY TWISTER WAS NEVER A POPULAR PRISON GAME.

"MY WIFE MISUNDERSTOOD ME WHEN I SAID 'I WAS GOING OUT TO PLAY A ROUND'."

JOHNSON HAD A HARD TIME COVERING THE SPREAD.

BOWLING PIN WAR STORIES

"... HE'S NOT VERY FAST, BUT IF THE RACE IS CLOSE..."

60

FRAZIER'S NEW MITT PROVIDED A TARGET PITCHERS COULD MORE EASILY CONCENTRATE ON.

THE SWIMSUIT EDITION OF SUMO WORLD
NEVER REALLY CAUGHT ON.

WHAT HAPPENS WHEN A CORPORATION NAMED **PETLAND** OWNS A BASEBALL TEAM.

"SURE HE'S A GREAT PLAYER, BUT HIS STABLE HOME LIFE GIVES HIS CARD LITTLE CHANCE OF APPRECIATION."

"LISTEN! I CALL 'EM LIKE I SEE 'EM."

BRAD WAS A TRUE SPORTSMAN

GOLFER, JOHN CARPENTER CAN USUALLY ONE-PUTT A GREEN.

73

SELDOM LOBBED, BUT OFTEN PASSED.

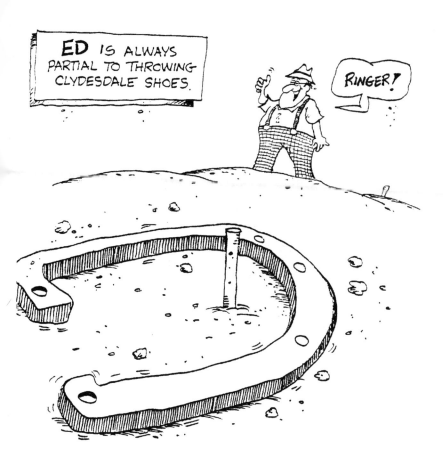

...WHY COWBOYS DON'T MAKE GOOD GOALIES.

" I TOLD YOU WE RUN A VERY COMPLICATED OFFENSE HERE. "

"SORRY, BUT I JUST GOT REALLY TIRED OF PLAYERS ACTING SO IMMATURE."

THOUGH THE WORDS 'BARBED WIRE' ARE NOT MENTIONED IN THE RULE BOOK— ED BAILEY HAS A GUT FEELING THIS IS AN ILLEGAL DEFENSE.

FRED HANDBURG IS WILLING TO GO TO ANY EXTREME TO BREAK INTO THE NBA.

"HOW CAN YOU BELIEVE THE LUNAR LANDINGS WERE FAKE AND THIS IS REAL ?"

"THAT'S WHAT HAPPENS WHEN RETAIL, CORPORATE
SPONSORSHIP CONTROLS A SPORTING EVENT."

NEVER DROP AN EASY FLY BALL— ON BAT DAY!

CALDWELL'S COLLEGE'S HOMECOMING GOT OFF TO A BAD
START WHEN LARRY LAMBERT, SET TO PARACHUTE IN
WITH THE GAME BALL ———————— FUMBLED!

"IF YOU THINK YOU HAVE SOME KNEE SURGERY SCARS— JUST TAKE A LOCK AT THAT BABY..."

"HE'S COUNTING BY 3's. ONE FOR EACH CHIN.

"THE FIRST HALF WAS SO DISASTEROUS FOR THE HOME TEAM, THE BAND IS SPELLING OUT S-O-S..."